WINSTON WINS

BY TIM A RUPARD

ILLUSTRATED BY

JONATHAN RUPARD
AND
TIM A RUPARD

PUBLISHED BY:

GOOD DOG READS PUBLISHING

Good Dog Reads
Publishing

VISIT US FOR THE WHOLE WINSTON STORY FOR ADULTS AT:
www.winstonstory.com

From the author:
I hope you are blessed by the book that has found its way into your hands. I truly believe the story that awaits you will shine love, hope, and peace into your life. The story is completely true. Winston is our family pet and is lying at my feet as I write this to you. He is healthy and full of joy! We have already begun visiting children in churches, and schools and hope to visit hospitals and nursing homes with Winston. He really owns a gold cape and he really jumps in dock dog competitions.

We genuinely believe God gave us a second chance to visit people and share this story of hope with them! We hope you enjoy our tale of a puppy, his family, and their fight against cancer.

Tim

Find us @ www.winstonstory.com

While this book is non-fiction and the story relayed is true, the author is not a professional medical worker.
He is not a professional preacher or faith healer.
The advice or ideas expressed within this book are not meant to replace the medical advice of doctors. The author believes that medical science definitely has its perfect place in the lives of people. If you or your loved ones are sick, seek medical attention while you pray for God's direction and healing. The named people have given permission to be named in the book.

Hey! My name is Winston. They call me Wincy for short! I was born in the springtime, when it was warm and flowers were starting to bloom! I had lots of brothers and sisters to snuggle with, while mama lay by our side!

1

One day, when I was two months old, a family came to adopt me and brought me to my new home! I was a little afraid at first, I missed mama, but soon I felt safe and knew this was where I belonged! There was Daddy Tim, Mama Karen, Sister Katy, and Sister Abby. There was also another one like me!
Her name was Heidi!

There were lots of things to do at my new home!

I chased balls and carried socks and I pestered Heidi and we played and played!

Heidi taught me lots of doggy things to do!

One of my favorite things that Heidi taught me, was to chase squirrels! One day, I almost caught one!

My whole family was amazing but
My Abby was the best!

She would let me sleep in her warm and
cozy bed! I felt safe and protected.

My Abby taught me lots of fun tricks,

Like how to sit

and how to stay.

How to walk on a leash

and how to lay!

Another favorite thing to do is what my Abby calls "Fetch!" She would throw a ball or a plastic bumper and I would run after it, grab it up and bring it back to her as fast as I could! It is a lot of fun! We played fetch over and over and over!

I love spending time with My Abby.

When I was two years old My Abby took me to a jumping pond for the very first time.

At first, I was scared to jump off the edge of the dock. I had never jumped into a clear pond before.

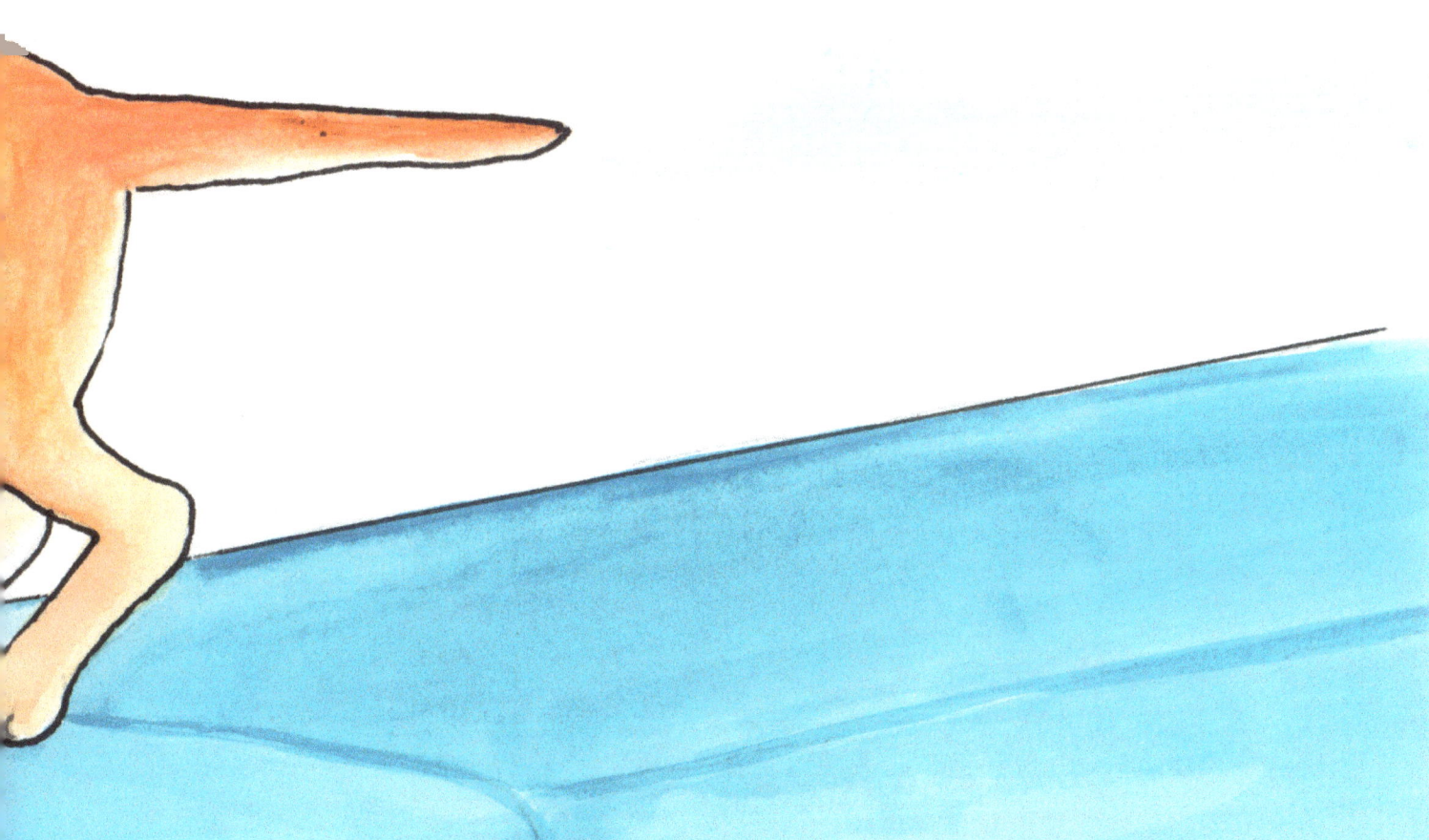

But, My Abby helped me to be brave and strong! She taught me how to jump high and long!

One day, Abby even entered us into a jumping competition for dogs. I was tail-wagging excited about competing, but Abby was really nervous for me, though she tried her best to hide it.

There were lots of other dogs there and I didn't know what to think of how they acted..

I decided, "I will jump so far! I'm not afraid! I'll make her so proud of me!"

I jumped so far, I jumped so high!
22 feet across the sky!

The crowd cheered loudly when I splashed into the water! Some of them yelled, "It's Winston, the Wonderdog!"
I could see Abby's face, she was so, so proud of me. She had no idea I could jump so far!

"Winston the Wonderdog!" She shouted with them.

I closed my eyes and imagined myself flying above the crowd, my golden cape flapping in the wind.
The people below me would look up and cheer, "It's Winston the Wonderdog! He has no fear!"

I won some fancy ribbons that day!

In one event, I even won first place!
My Abby was so amazed.

We hung them proudly
in our room for all to see!
I was happy I had made her proud of me.

I loved jumping and training with Abby, it made me happy to be with her. But when I wasn't training with Abby, I was playing with my best doggy friend Heidi!

Sniffing, exploring, running and hiding,
and our favorite,
tug-o-war!

Suddenly, one day my leg started hurting.
It hurt really bad.

I wanted to run and play with Heidi or
fetch with Abby, but it just hurt too
much!

So, Daddy Tim took me to the Doctor. It was kind of scary but they were really nice to me. The Vet checked my heartbeat and took my temperature. Then, she took some really neat pictures of my bones, called an X-ray.

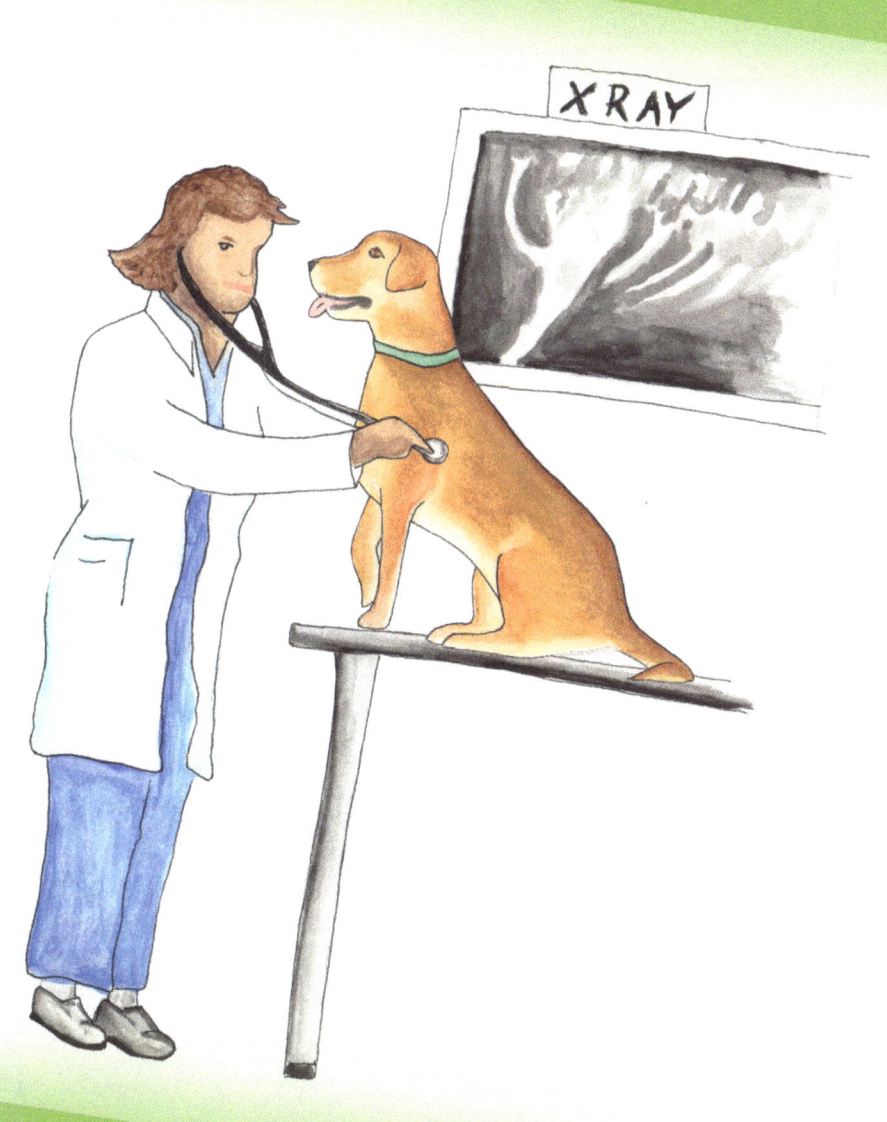

After that, they said I had something called cancer in my bone. She told Daddy Tim it was really bad and there wasn't much they could do. Then she said I was going to die! That seemed to make Daddy Tim very sad.

I was confused. They were all crying so much. I just knew my leg was hurting! I couldn't walk. I had to lay around or hop, hop, hop, everywhere I went!

At first, I think everyone thought something terrible was going to happen to me, but Daddy Tim thought something different. He kept saying "I believe God told me Winston would live! I don't care what the Doctors say, he is going to be just fine!" My family and friends began to believe what Daddy Tim was saying too! They made me brave, but all I knew was my leg still hurt!

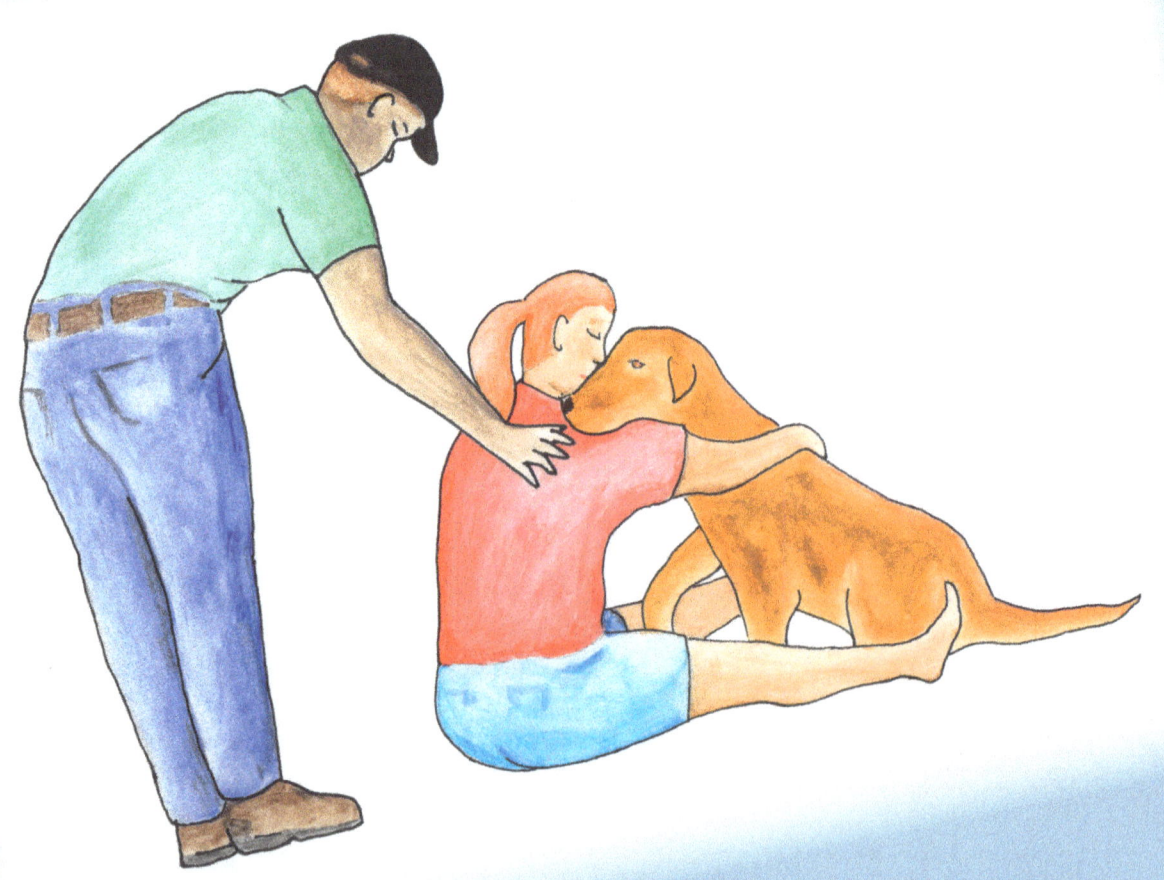

My family would sit with me on the floor and put their hands on me. They would close their eyes and pray to God, asking Him to heal me. I didn't really understand all of it, but it felt so good to be loved like that!

They prayed everyday. Even when it seemed like it wasn't working.

I had to take yucky medicine too! I didn't like it. Even Daddy Tim's socks tasted better! They said it was for my pain, but it didn't help much.
I did like the pepperonis they would wrap it in though!

It seemed like I was just getting worse. Some days, it hurt so bad, all I could do was lay there.

I even laid on the couch in Daddy Tim's office. He never let me lay there before I was sick!

One day, something happened. I guess it was all that praying...

I went outside and my leg just started feeling better!

I started walking normal again. My leg didn't hurt anymore AT ALL!
I tested it out in the yard with Daddy Tim. It didn't even hurt to fetch!

I started playing again!
I ran, and jumped, and ran some more! I was feeling like my old doggy self again!

I can run and jump and swim again!
It's a miracle!
I am so happy that God healed me!
It's hard to believe, but I am cancer free!

I didn't understand how this could be,
Daddy Tim keeps saying,
"God answered our prayers, He loves us
and cares for us!"
And I guess He really does!

I know some kids feel just like I did. I wondered if God would heal me because I am just a puppy! But Daddy Tim keeps saying, "If it's important to you, it's important to God!" So, when you are feeling sick and sad, and it hurts really bad, just remember, I've been there too...

I pray that God will heal everyone who is sick, especially you!

If Winston the Wonderdog can win, so can you!
God healed Wincy, He can heal you too!

THE END

www.ingramcontent.com/pod-product-compliance
Lightning Source LLC
Chambersburg PA
CBHW041155120626
46547CB00020B/3229